Anxiety Workbook

Compiled by Don Boice, LCSW-R

585.802.1273

We put together some ways to cope, borrowing from modern psychology, some spiritual traditions and just common sense. These are tools you can use any time, night or day.

It is your job to soothe yourself, to calm yourself down. You have more power when you can do this yourself. You are less dependent on others when you take on this responsibility.

Before you ask someone else for help calming or self-soothing, try one of these. After you have helped yourself, ask for help making it even more effective. But try it yourself first.

We have also recorded three separate CDs. One with letting go and another with relaxation techniques. Get to know them so that when you need help calming down, you know where to go. There is a third one that comes from ideas for this workbook.

Feelings

We have given too much credence to feelings in our culture. Feelings are not facts, they are merely bodily sensations. We create them in our heads in reaction to what we interpret in the outside world. We do not have to feel anxious. We do not have to create fear with our brains. We can create whatever we want. Stop creating anxiety and create something different.

Let's look at the concept of Independent Origination

Where do feelings originate? Do they float through the ethers and land in our psyche?

No, we create feelings. They do not happen to us; we create them. The joy in this is that when we do not like the way we feel, we can change it.

There is no independent origination. The feeling cannot exist without an interpretation, a perspective being taken. That is where we have control. There are multiple perspectives for any situation; therefore there are multiple options for feelings.

The feelings you have right now are not the only option. If you feel wronged, figure out what is in your control and change what you are able to change. Let go of the rest or you will drive yourself crazy. (Letting Go is the theme of one of the CDs. Get familiar with it. It is nearly impossible to be both anxious and to let go.)

Do not perceive that your mental health is dependent on the actions of others. You give away altogether much too much control when you do that and usually end up feeling worse.

Ultimately, your solution is within. Even if you did not cause the problem, do not feel you brought it on yourself, your solution is within. Think of the person who was abused. They still have to deal with the results of it. Complaining about that does not improve the situation. Coming to a better understanding of it, looking at it from multiple perspectives is what helps. Getting stuck in a perspective does not help. "Well, they should not have abused me," he said. While that is true, it is a short-term perspective. Now, what are you going to do with that?

I can handle just about anything. So can you, you just do not realize it yet.

What are some good coping skills to learn?

The alphabet soup of counseling offers us skills from the follow CBT, DBT, RET, EFT.

I can have opposite reactions and I can break patterns by changing how I respond, rehearsing it and practicing it over and over.

I can even just tap right hand, then left hand on my legs and concentrate on my body. You can change your position. If you are sitting down, you can stand up and walk around.

SELF STATEMENTS

Let's start with the cornerstone of counseling, how we talk to ourselves.

- I can handle this.
- This is inconvenient, that is all.
- I can do this.
- I accept the blessings that come with this pain.
- I look for the lesson in all of this.
- I can cope with this in a healthy manner.
- No one is to blame for my feelings; I am responsible for how I feel, though.
- Feelings are not facts.
- Feelings change and I can ride the wave.

- This feeling will pass.
- There are other ways to look at this and I will explore at least three more before I decide how I want to feel.
- I fill my own emptiness.
- I may not have the best perspective on this situation.
- I will see if there is evidence to support my point of view or if I am simply overreacting to this.
- It is possible that I do not see this clearly.
- I allow myself to heal quickly from this by letting go and moving on.
- I allow myself to let go and get on with my life.
- No one has to prove anything to me and I have nothing to prove to them.
- I release my obsessing and ruminating and racing thoughts.
- I release, I let go of, blind spots on this issue.
- I can be okay inside, even if nothing external changes.
- I let go of my preferences and my control of this situation.
- I accept that the situation may not change and I only have control of my reaction to the situation.
- I need to stop thinking about this or I risk becoming self absorbed and self indulgent.
- I see this situation through God's eyes.
- I come at this situation from a position of love, there is nothing more powerful.
- There is nothing that needs to change.
- I grow closer to wholeness when I allow life to be as it is and not poke at the emotions.
- I see this situation through the eyes of my higher self.
- Nature does not operate independently of what we think, wish, dream and feel.
- Do not heed voices of fear or guilt.
- There is no action more important than surrender.

In Rational Emotive Therapy (Albert Ellis) we learn:

The event does not cause the suffering. The event might cause pain, our interpretation of the event is what causes the suffering. This is not to blame, it is to find causes and roots. Some people really dislike this because it places the responsibility for their feelings directly on their shoulders and they fully believe they are a victim of the circumstance.

You are not to blame for your circumstances, you are however responsible for finding your way out. If you rely on someone else to get you out of them, you may be waiting quite some time.

Imagine the person who finds themselves really upset that a certain event happened. The event happened, no matter what their reaction to it. The event may have been terrible, horrific even. We have compassion for them.

They are ultimately responsible for getting out of the suffering, though. No one else can do it for them. Someone else can hold their hand while they get out, or give suggestions or coach from the sidelines, but they must do the work of looking at their thoughts, disputing them, challenging them, changing their reactions, their breathing, their posture, challenging motivation etc.

The worst coping mechanism is trying to change the world instead of changing my self or my perspective. Marsha Linehan has written a bunch on this topic of Radical Acceptance. How do I accept something that I frankly find unacceptable? It does not mean I condone it, justify it or think it is okay, I simply change my relationship with it.

You cannot change it and trying to change anything or anyone else is futile. Heck, even the changes within ourselves are a challenge!

If you are relying on something outside yourself to do the changing, you are creating part two of a problem.

"I can only be okay if _________________________ happens," you might think. That thinking is harmful to you and your ability to cope.

If I am not in harmony with the world, I can either ask the world to change or I can change. My money is on you changing- the odds are much better.

Looking at Cognitive Behavioral Theory by Aaron Beck, Martin Seligman wrote:

How do we see bad events?

Optimist		*Pessimist*
This sometimes happens. The cause is changeable or transient.	<u>Permanence</u>	This always happens this way. The cause is something that will persist.
This specific thing is bad. The cause will affect only a few situations.	<u>Pervasiveness</u>	Everything is bad. This cause will affect many situations.
This behavior is not good. The cause is something about other people or circumstances.	<u>Personal</u>	My personality or character is to blame. I am the cause.

An OPTIMIST would think to herself, "I got a C on the test because I did not study hard enough" -this stems from a belief that it is temporary, specific and the blame is internal.

A PESSIMIST would think to herself, "I got a C on the test because I am stupid" - she thinks that is it permanent, pervasive and the blame is internal.

Blaming failure on poor ability is pessimistic therefore undermines trying.

Blaming failure on trying, lack of effort, not paying attention etc. is optimistic and changeable.

Again, it is how we look at what happens that is most often the most critical part of the equation. That is not to minimize that trauma can happen and override the brain. Trauma is disruptive to your body and mind.

Martin Seligman also wrote about the following:

Challenging how you explain things to yourself (Disputation)

I. Thought Catching- when you notice you feel badly, ask yourself, "What thoughts just crossed my mind?"

II. Evaluating automatic thoughts- beliefs about myself and the world are hypotheses that need to be tested. Pessimistic beliefs often are not accurate, they are just the first things that pop into our head. "Hot thoughts" make us react instead of respond. Slow down when you have one of these and realize the other person probably did not do it "on purpose."

III. Generating more accurate explanations- Is how I look at it the only possible explanation? What are other ways of viewing this situation? What is the evidence that my thinking is making it worse right now?

IV. It is not a catastrophe- What are the worst and best *possible* outcomes? How likely are each? Now, what can I do to improve the situation?

Got that? Now you can prepare for quicker disputing of negative thoughts so that you can view yourself as accurately as possible.

ABC

Adversities (A) Beliefs (B) and their Consequences (C)

If you firmly held this belief about the adversity, you would feel and act in a specific way.

A Your spouse has been distant and distracted lately

B You think __________________ (fill in the blanks)

C You become increasingly irritable with her/him and notice yourself picking fights.

Fill in the thoughts you would have to think to make you feel irritable. Remember that while the facts matter, how someone *interprets* facts matters the most.

If B is "He has no right to take his moods out on me" then you would likely feel some sort of anger or irritability.

If you interpret his distance as a sign that he is losing interest in you, then sadness might be the consequence.

DBT

Thank you to Marsha Linehan for systematizing the coping techniques. We have been using the techniques for years and she made them much easier to use.

Each of the following is a mnemonic device. The letters of the first word are spelled out and this helps us memorize the tools

EMOTIONS
E xposure yourself to the emotion,
M indful of current emotions,
O utline plan to deal,
T ake opposite action,
I ncrease positive experiences,
O utside precipitants,
N otice what is going on,
S econdary emotions deal with

If you were having a rough day, and I suggested you try to apply EMOTIONS to it, what would you do?

1. Stop avoiding the anxiety. Feel the feeling, not in an effort to get rid of it. Go with the flow.
2. Get to know the feeling of anxiety. It is a creation of your mind. Pay attention to it. Perhaps it has a lesson for you.
3. Figure out how you are going to deal with the anxiety (face it with EMOTIONS)
4. Do something that makes you feel happy so as to shut down the gate of anxiety
5. Think of a time that you felt happy and carefree. Run that through your mind a few times.

6. Consider how it is you got to this level of anxiety so that you can interrupt it sooner next time.
7. Pay attention to how you created it, how you lived through it and that both your body and your brain paid attention to where your mind focused.
8. Deal with the emotions that came up after you felt anxious.

Distress tolerance

DISTRACT

D o something else- something that absorbs you

I mages- bring up compelling images from your past

S ense- You have 5 senses, use them all

T hink about something you enjoy

R emember your happy moments from your past

A ccept your current situation, change what is in your power to change

C reate a new meaning to this

T ake opposite action- do something that shuts down that part of your brain

VISION

V ision- pay attention right now to what you see

I magery is very good to get you distracted or ground you

S oothing- it is your job to calm yourself down, soothe yourself

I nspiration- what inspires you? Have it ready for these situations

O ne thing at a time- multi tasking is not desirable – be in the moment

N otice- be aware of what is happening right here, right now

Discriminate primary from secondary emotions

I feel hurt and vulnerable. Pay attention to those first. As you resolve those, notice that other feelings are also there. One at a time, process your feelings.

What are feelings?

Emotions are for survival- must be acknowledged and experienced

Avoidance of them makes them stronger

Feelings are a form of sensing the world like your other 5 senses

Feelings are not facts

Four Helpful Thoughts

1. Want to be rich? Those who need the least are the richest. Think about those whose needs are few. Their needs are met and they feel content, satisfied. Ask yourself, "Is it possible what you think of as a "need" is a "want?" Ask yourself, "Is this in my best interest?" Those with fewer needs seem to be happier.

2. Want to be happy? Do what happy people do; don't pursue your own happiness. Happiness is a by-product of serving others, of bringing happiness to others, of doing virtuous things, of having compassion. A happy mind is very peaceful.

3. Want to be liberated? Remind yourself that you alone cause your feelings. If you cause your own feelings, you are also responsible for changing how you feel. If you are miserable, you have the ability to make yourself not miserable. Think of happy thoughts and happy times and put yourself in a good mood and watch how you attract good things to you. What is the return on your investment? Happiness and liberation

   Focus on the solution and you attract that. Focus on the problem and you attract that.

4. Want less suffering? The desire for things to be different than what they are is the biggest cause of suffering. Offer no resistance to life as it is. Change nothing except your resistance. Criticism diminishes the criticizer. Emerge into who you are, being at one with yourself. Let go completely and, by definition, your struggle ends.

Emotional Freedom Technique

What is it?

EFT is a tapping technique created by Gary Craig, a Minister, who also trained as an Engineer at Stanford. He was interested in alleviating suffering as quickly as possible. While it may look a little strange at first, it works beautifully. You just might not want to do it in public. It involves lightly stimulating acupuncture points while we focus on emotions, issues or concerns. Once these blocks are cleared, your healing naturally follows and your energy level returns to normal.

You rub or tap points on your body that help distract your brain, keep you focused and the points themselves are based on acupuncture points that deal with specific emotions.

You can tap one or two emotions or the whole lot of them. Acupuncture has been around roughly 2,500 years and is used for physical as well as emotional ailments with great success. In Chinese Medicine, they talk about meridians and that any blocks in your meridian will cause disease at some level. Clearing the blocks and returning the flow of energy is the start of returning to full health.

You will find that EFT is usually quite gentle and you can often achieve substantial relief with no pain. There are also no co-pays for doing this yourself. You do not have to rely on others to talk or be there at 3 am when you need relief.

EFT can be used for anything, including physical discomforts and allergies, or to improve sports performance, to overcome all kinds of emotional issues and more.

Who can do it?

Anyone can use EFT and you don't need specialized schooling for it. In most cases, common sense will do. No meds or surgeries involved either.

To Start

So, at the beginning of each treatment, we identify an issue. To do this, we either rub on the sore spot or tap on the karate chop point while saying, "Even though I have this problem (and you name the problem), I deeply and completely love and accept myself." For example, you might say, "Even though I always feel as there is never enough, I deeply and completely love and accept myself."

Or, "Even though my parents always told me that I'd never be rich, I deeply and completely love and accept myself." With this one, you might add "and I forgive my parents for what they said."

Ok, first is the spot on the inside of the eyebrow. Not between the eyes, but just at the beginning of your eyebrow (you should feel bone). Tap that a few times. Next is the spot on the outside of the eyebrow (follow the bone). Tap Tap Tap. You can do this on either side of your body. Don't pound on the spots, just tap them. The next spot is under your eye (follow that bone).

Next is just under the nose, above the lip. Tap tap tap, then between your mouth and chin, in that indentation, just below your lip. Tap tap tap.

Next is the collarbone spot. First find the end of the collarbone on each side. Using your thumb and index finger, you'll find two bumps, one on either side of your body, just below the middle of your neck. Can you feel the two bumps? These are what I'm calling the end of the collarbone.

The last point on the body is under your arm. You'll have to lift your arm for this one. It's a few inches below your armpit. You might not want to do these in public.

These are the points that we use **most of the time**. But sometimes, we use some additional ones, which I'll show you now.

Second Series of Points

First, let's do the points on your hand. Tap just on the outside edge (not the edge facing your other fingers) of the skin right next to your thumbnail. Tap tap tap, the same place on your index finger, the same place on your middle finger, and then the same place on your pinky.

The last spot on the hand is what is called the karate chop point. It's on the bottom edge of your hand. Just tap this with the fingers of your other hand, palm open. (So you'll be hitting it with more than two fingers.) Remember we are doing tapping now, but you can also rub/massage the points.

The last spot

It's on the back of your hand, between your pinky and ring finger and back away from the knuckle about an inch toward the wrist. We call this the gamut point. It's used for what is called the nine gamut exercise, which we only use on occasion as a *brain balancer*. I'll tell you about that when I take you through a treatment.

Prosperity Session

I'm going to pick an issue that often comes up for people who are doing prosperity work. If you don't think it applies to you, then when we are saying the phrases, you can just say something that applies to you.

Let's do one for "I don't deserve to be wealthy." This belief is often present when people are working to create financial comfort. They might say they deserve it, but underneath is that reversal that says, you don't deserve it.

Start by closing your eyes and thinking about the statement "I don't deserve to be wealthy." What kind of feelings does saying that to yourself bring up for you? Think of yourself as always struggling financially. Can you see that picture? As you go into that feeling, think about where you are feeling discomfort. Then decide, on a scale of 0 to 10, 0 being none and 10 being awful, how intense the discomfort is.

Now let's do it
Rub the sore spot on your chest while you say,

"Even though I don't deserve to be wealthy and I feel that no matter how hard I try I'll never be wealthy, I deeply and completely love and accept myself." Again
"Even though I don't deserve to be wealthy and I feel that no matter how hard I try I'll never be wealthy, I deeply and completely love and accept myself."
And again,
"Even though I don't deserve to be wealthy and I feel that no matter how hard I try I'll never be wealthy, I deeply and completely love and accept myself." (3 times total)

Now, as we tap on the other points, let's use the reminder phrase, "don't deserve wealth." Remember, you'll tap about seven to ten times. There is nothing bad that will happen with 6 or 11, just 7-10 have been found to be most effective.
Tap inside your eyebrow as you day "don't deserve wealth"
Now outside your eyebrow tap tap tap "don't deserve wealth"
Under your eye "don't deserve wealth"
Under your nose "don't deserve wealth"
On your chin "don't deserve wealth"
The collarbone point "don't deserve wealth
Under your arms "don't deserve wealth"
Outside edge of thumbnail "don't deserve wealth
Index finger "don't deserve wealth
Middle finger "don't deserve wealth
Pinky "don't deserve wealth

Now, Tap on the gamut point on the back of your hand while you follow these instructions
Close your eyes
Open your eyes
Look hard right down, keeping your head still
Look hard left down, keeping your head still
Make a circle with your eyes, keeping your head still
Make a circle in the opposite direction, keeping your head still
Look straight ahead and Hum the first five notes of happy birthday (hum)
Count quickly to five "1 2 3 4 5"
Hum the first five notes of happy birthday.

Now we are going to do one more tapping round.
Tap inside your eyebrow as you day "still don't deserve wealth"
Now outside your eyebrow tap tap tap "still don't deserve wealth"
Under your eye "still don't deserve wealth"
Under your nose "don't deserve wealth"
On your chin "don't deserve wealth"
The collarbone point "don't deserve wealth
Under your arms "don't deserve wealth"
Outside edge of thumbnail "don't deserve wealth
Index finger "don't deserve wealth:
Middle finger "don't deserve wealth"
Pinky "don't deserve wealth"

Ok. Close your eyes and take a deep breath.

Go inside again and think about not deserving wealth. Give the discomfort
a number from 0 to 10. Is it less than it was at the very beginning of doing
this? Chances are that it is. If there is still discomfort, you can go through
this again and tap some more. Then, take a reading again as to where you
are with this.

There's a good chance that other issues will come up while you are doing
this. You can treat any of the issues as they come up and try to get them
down close to a zero.

Alternate ways to tap:

There is a point at the top of your head, your crown. Lightly tap with 3-4
fingers 7-10 times before the eyebrow point.

Also, many people have added tapping your wrists together.

Common practice is to tap with both hands at each point around the eyes.
Try it and see if you like that approach.

What else to say while you are tapping:

You can create whatever you would like and tap to that. There are some more powerful things to say, though. You can say one thing over and over or you can say something different with each point, stay on the same topic, and just say different aspects of it. See the YouTube for ideas on that.

"Why does money come so easily to me?" "I am grateful that money flows to me so easily." People have found wonderful results with these. In the first, you ask the question "Why does" and then you fill in whatever the problem is, stated as a positive. This person struggled with feeling abundant. The second statement phrases it as a grateful and found it really helped her. "I am grateful that…" and then state the positive affirmation. Try it and experiment with the wording and pay attention to the feeling that it produces while you are actually tapping

While you are tapping, you generally think about the negative and it will be explained in the brain section why we do this.

Brain Issues:

Someone who knows more about the brain than I talked about implications of this for the brain. The brain cannot entertain two simultaneous thoughts of equal charge. If you are having really negative thoughts and you introduce a positive thought, you brain bumps the weaker one out. When you have a negative thought, start tapping and saying it and thinking the thought, the intensity of the negative reduces significantly increasing the likelihood that the positive thoughts in your head at that time will bump out the negative.

In the gamut spot, you are doing some interesting things with your brain, as well. When you close and open your eyes, it can function as a reset. It can reset your brain. For those of us who think too much, this is a welcome thing. Looking down to one side stimulates the opposite side of the brain. They you switch sides that you are looking which stimulates the other side of the brain. Then you integrate left and right hemispheres of the brain by rolling eyes in a circle. (One side of brain does emotion, the other does intellect- consider the advantage of having the two of them communicating.) When you hum, you are in the musical part of the brain, then counting puts you in the mathematical part, and then you hum again. Think now of all the parts of the brain that you stimulated. How hard is it to obsess when you have engaged that much of your brain? Sure, you can do it, but for how long?

Side effects:

Some people start crying when they do this. This is not a bad thing, they are releasing energy, that is all. If this thought scares you, please do not do it yourself, do it with a therapist who knows this technique and walk through it with them.

The other very common side effect is tiredness. People realize how tired they are, how much they have been carrying with them. Some people start yawning a lot and get sleepy. So do not drive if you have been tapping more than 10-15 minutes. Get up, move around, wake yourself up, and then resume your day.

By the way, it works wonders for insomnia due to this side effect.

Each point and the feelings it relates to:

(If you do not like how you are feeling and this is your feeling, tap this specific point)

- Tap inside your eyebrow   Restlessness, impatience, frustration
- Now outside your eyebrow   Rage, furry, wrath
- Under your eye   Anxiety, disgust, bitterness, disappointment, greed, hunger, deprivation
- Under your nose   Embarrassment
- On your chin (under the lip) Shame
- The collarbone point   Anxiety, sexual indecision
- Under your arms   Anxiety
- Outside edge of thumbnail Disdain, scorn, contempt, intolerance, prejudice
- Index finger   Guilt
- Middle finger   Regret, remorse, jealousy, sexual tension, stubbornness

- Pinky   Anger
- Karate chop   Sadness, sorrow
- 9 gamut   Depression, despair, grief, hopelessness, despondence, loneliness

Check out the follow websites for YouTube you may enjoy:

David Childerly www.myGenie.tv (UK)

Or www.EFT-Practice.com

NOTE: many people are not using the psychological reversals and that is okay. They work when you find a stuck point. *If you sabotage yourself at all, you probably have a psychological reversal.*

Psychological Reversals

Compiled from Thought Field Therapy

Read the following statements and instead of saying to yourself, "THIS PROBLEM" interject the actual problem. For example, "I deserve to be completely over my excessive jealousy in this relationship." The more specific, the better your brain responds.

After you read **each** statement, answer the question, *"How does that feel?"*:

Top section:

I deserve to be completely over THIS PROBLEM. (For example, jealousy)

I deserve to still have some of THIS PROBLEM.

Deep in my unconscious, it is safe for me to be completely over THIS PROBLEM.

It is possible for me to be completely over THIS PROBLEM.

I will allow myself to completely get over THIS PROBLEM.

I will do what is necessary to completely get over THIS PROBLEM.

Getting completely over THIS PROBLEM will be good for me.

I will not feel deprived if I completely get over THIS PROBLEM.

Note: Pay attention to which one (s) stood out in terms of difficulty. Some are harder than others to say. You feel it in your gut or it has a hard time coming out of your mouth. The ones that are hard to say are the ones that you need to work on the most. Notice below that each one of these corresponds to the group above. For example, *if you stumbled over the one that included "safety" in the top section, you would look for the corresponding one in the bottom section and say that out loud.* Figure out which one sounds better to you. Talk about this with your counselor to go even deeper.

Bottom section:

I deeply accept myself even if I deserve to have THIS PROBLEM.

I deeply accept myself even if I deserve to have some of THIS PROBLEM.

I deeply accept myself even if it is not safe for me to be completely over THIS PROBLEM.

I deeply accept myself even if it's impossible for me to get completely over THIS PROBLEM.

I deeply accept myself even if I will not allow myself to get completely over THIS PROBLEM.

I deeply accept myself even though I will not do what is necessary to get completely over THIS PROBLEM.

I deeply accept myself even though getting completely over THIS PROBLEM will not be good for me.

I deeply accept myself even if I might be deprived if I get over THIS PROBLEM.